Young
Amelia Earhart

A Dream to Fly

A Troll First-Start® Biography

by Sarah Alcott
illustrated by James Anton

Troll Associates

Library of Congress Cataloging-in-Publication Data

Alcott, Sarah.
   Young Amelia Earhart: a dream to fly / by Sarah Alcott;
illustrated by James Anton.
     p.   cm.—(First-start biographies)
   Summary: A simple biography of the pilot who became the first
woman to fly alone across the Atlantic Ocean.
   ISBN 0-8167-2528-4 (lib. bdg.)   ISBN 0-8167-2529-2 (pbk.)
   1. Earhart, Amelia, 1897-1937—Juvenile literature. 2. Air
pilots—United States—Biography—Juvenile literature.
[1. Earhart, Amelia, 1897-1937. 2. Air pilots.] I. Anton, James,
ill. II. Title. III. Series.
TL540.E3A73 1992
629.13 '092—dc20
[B]   91-24974

This edition published in 2002.

Amelia Earhart was America's
greatest woman pilot. Her daring
adventures made her famous all
over the world.

Amelia was born in Kansas in 1897.
In those days, girls had to act like
ladies. They could not play games
like boys did.

But Amelia and her younger sister
Muriel were lucky. Their mother and
father believed girls and boys should
be treated the same.

Amelia and Muriel were allowed to play baseball, football, and other sports. Amelia loved to think of exciting games to play.

One winter day Amelia, Muriel, and
their friends went sledding. But just
as Amelia was zooming down a big
hill, a large, horse-drawn wagon
crossed the street in front of her.

The driver did not see Amelia. And there was no time for Amelia to stop. But Amelia was calm. She steered the sled *underneath* the horse!

Amelia saw her first airplane at the
Iowa State Fair when she was 11
years old. She did not know then
that one day airplanes would change
her life.

When Amelia grew up, she worked as a nurse. One day Amelia and a friend saw some pilots doing tricks in the air. As she watched the planes turn and dive, Amelia got very excited.

"I must learn to fly," Amelia said.
And so she began taking lessons.

Amelia learned everything about planes. She could even take an engine apart and put it back together!

17

Amelia learned how to fly in all kinds
of weather. Her teacher taught her to
fly at night, too.

Finally, after practicing for a long time, Amelia got her pilot's license. She was 25 years old.

Soon Amelia became the greatest
woman pilot in the world.

In 1932, Amelia flew across
the Atlantic Ocean by herself.
No woman had ever done that.

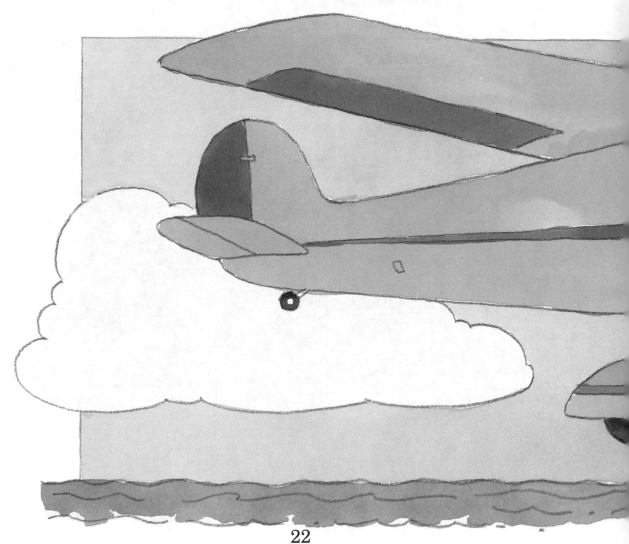

Amelia set many records in her
little plane. People all over the
world cheered her on.

In 1937, Amelia decided to do
something no one had ever done
before. She wanted to fly around
the world.

She and a man named Fred Noonan
began their around-the-world
adventure in Miami, Florida.

For a month, everything went well.
Then Amelia and Fred headed for
Howland Island in the Pacific Ocean.

But something went wrong. Amelia
and Fred never arrived at Howland
Island. And no one ever heard from
them again.

No one knows what happened to Amelia Earhart. Most people think her plane crashed in the ocean.

But Amelia has never been forgotten. Her brave spirit and exciting adventures still inspire people today.

Index